Protecting Our Planet

What Can We Do About POLLUTION?

Suzanne Slade

PowerKiDS press.

New York

To my clever clean-up crew: Kellie, Hal, Tina, Dawn,
Anne, Jeff M., Jeff E., Shawn, Roger, and Lorijo

Published in 2010 by The Rosen Publishing Group, Inc.
29 East 21st Street, New York, NY 10010

First Edition

Editor: Amelie von Zumbusch
Book Design: Kate Laczynski
Photo Researcher: Jessica Gerweck

Photo Credits: Cover, p. 1 Mark Horn/Getty Images; back cover graphic © www.istockphoto.com/Jan Rysavy; p. 4 L. Lefkowitz/Getty Images; pp. 6, 14 Shutterstock.com; p. 8 Oxford Scientific/Photolibrary/Getty Images; p. 10 Alan Levenson/Getty Images; p. 12 Paul Grebliunas/Getty Images; p. 16 Ben Osborne/Getty Images; p. 18 © Amanda Hall/Robert Harding World Imagery/Corbis; p. 20 © George Steinmetz/Corbis.

Library of Congress Cataloging-in-Publication Data

Slade, Suzanne.
  What can we do about pollution? / Suzanne Slade.
     p. cm. — (Protecting our planet)
  Includes index.
  ISBN 978-1-4042-8083-0 (lib. bdg.) — ISBN 978-1-4358-2485-0 (pbk.) — ISBN 978-1-4358-2486-7 (6-pack)
  1. Pollution—Juvenile literature. I. Title.
  TD176.S58 2010
  363.73—dc22
                                    2008053822

Manufactured in China

CONTENTS

Sometimes, pollution is easy to see. This stream is polluted with an orange scum that floats on top of the water.

What Is Pollution?

The beautiful Earth is our home. However, people produce waste that pollutes our world. Cars and factories give off gases that make the air dirty. Oil from boats pollutes our waters. The **chemicals** that farmers use to help crops grow pollute the land and water. Littering also pollutes lakes and oceans, as well as our land.

Pollution hurts plants, animals, and people. Today, we are searching for ways to make less pollution. Many people are **recycling** their trash. Others are cleaning up polluted rivers and streams. People are deciding to walk or ride their bikes instead of using their cars, too. By working together, we can make our world a cleaner place to live.

Cars, like these ones on a California highway, cause smog. Smog, or polluted fog, makes it hard for people to breathe.

Dirty Air

Both people and nature make air pollution. Strong winds blow dirt up in the air. Forest fires produce thick smoke. People burn **fuel** to run cars and factories and to heat houses. Burning fuels give off gases that pollute the air. Air pollution can hurt our **lungs** and cause illnesses.

Many people are fighting air pollution. Carmakers are building new cars that produce less air pollution. Factories are buying newer machines that make less pollution. Some power plants are using special **filters** to trap pollution before it leaves their tall chimneys. All these efforts are making our air cleaner.

Acid Rain

Air pollution can also end up in our water. Cars and other machines give off gases that join **water vapor** in the air. This mixture becomes **acid** rain. Acid rain wears away the metal on cars, bridges, and railroad tracks. It eats away at stone buildings.

Acid rain can kill trees and other plants. It hurts leaves and washes **nutrients** that plants need out of the soil. Acid rain is a danger to every plant and animal in an ecosystem. An ecosystem is all the plants and animals that live in a certain place. For example, acid rain falls into lakes and kills fish. Animals that eat fish, such as eagles and bears, might not have enough food.

This man is helping clean up an oil spill in Alaska. The red oil boom next to his boat keeps oil from spreading any farther.

What's in Our Water?

Acid rain is just one of the many things that pollute our water. Factories use water to cool and clean their machines. This water often becomes full of chemicals that are unsafe for living things. In our homes, we pollute water with soap, shampoo, and human waste.

All living things, from mockingbirds to mountain goats, need clean water to drink. Polluted water can make people and animals sick. Government groups such as the Environmental Protection Agency, or EPA, work to clean up polluted water in the United States. These groups also help stop new water pollution.

DID YOU KNOW?

In 1972, it became illegal for U.S. farmers to use DDT, a chemical that kills bugs. Before that, DDT had washed into lakes. It killed fish and animals, such as birds, that eat fish.

Hazardous Waste

Hazardous waste is a type of pollution that can be a huge danger to people. This waste requires special care. People produce some hazardous wastes, such as **batteries** and bug sprays, at home. These should not be thrown away in the trash. Learn how to safely get rid of them from your trash service.

Another kind of hazardous waste, called **radioactive** waste, comes from power plants that make nuclear **energy**. Nuclear energy is energy that comes from breaking **atoms** apart. This waste is kept in strong vats lined with steel. Radioactive waste is stored far away from people.

DID YOU KNOW?

Certain lightbulbs in homes, schools, and businesses are also hazardous waste. Old lightbulbs must be handled carefully and many can be recycled!

14

Many brownfields are mills that have shut down. The EPA has helped clean up the land around hundreds of old mills across the United States

Pollution in Communities

Many towns have businesses, such as dry cleaners, factories, paper mills, or gas stations, that pollute the land around them. This polluted land is called a brownfield. Once a business leaves a brownfield, this empty land cannot be used until it is cleaned up.

Although it is costly to clean a brownfield, many communities are doing so. For example, the Atlantic Steel mill ran for over 80 years in Atlanta, Georgia. After the mill closed, the land around it was a brownfield. This land was later cleaned and renamed Atlantic Station. Today it holds new houses, offices, hotels, and parks. Pittsburgh, Pennsylvania, and Seattle, Washington, have also been very successful at cleaning up and finding new uses for brownfields.

Scientists measure how much of the gas oxygen is in rivers. Fish need oxygen, but pollution causes some rivers to have too little oxygen in them.

Studying Pollution

Many **scientists** are trained to study pollution. They measure different kinds of pollution and search for answers to this growing problem. Scientists check for acid rain by measuring pH. A lower pH number means the water is more acidic. Fish, frogs, and other animals often die if they live in water that has too low a pH.

To learn about air pollution, some scientists have taken to the sky! Planes with special labs allow scientists to test chemicals in the air. This helps scientists discover what is polluting the air. Scientists also track air pollution to find out how it travels.

Pollution Laws

Many governments are making laws to fight pollution. For example, the United States, Canada, and other countries have passed laws that are known as Clean Air Acts. These laws limit the amount of pollution that cars, factories, and other businesses can put in the air. The United States also has a Clean Water Act that makes sure our water stays safe and clean. For example, it tells companies, such as carmakers, how much pollution they are allowed to let into our waters.

While some pollution laws are written for big businesses, other laws are made for people. For example, new laws make it illegal to smoke in workplaces and other public buildings. These laws keep our inside air clean, too!

People Fighting Pollution

Governments, lawmakers, and scientists help lower our pollution, but it is important for each person to fight pollution, too. You can make your neighborhood cleaner by trying a few simple things.

Keep your water cleaner by learning the safe way to get rid of old paint and cleaners instead of pouring them down the sink. Gather a group of friends to pick up trash in your yard and nearby parks. To cut down on air pollution, you can walk or ride your bike instead of taking the car. If we each do our part, our communities will be cleaner and healthier for everyone.

DID YOU KNOW?

Recycling newspaper, cans, and bottles helps fight pollution. Recycling cuts down the amount of waste we make. About one-third of the waste from American homes is recycled.

Keeping Earth clean is everyone's job. Governments and communities fight pollution in different ways, but together they can accomplish great things. For example, the United States' Superfund **program** helps clean up hazardous waste. A community group in South Carolina worked with Superfund to clean up chemical and radioactive wastes a factory had dumped near the Savannah River. Together, they cleaned up land and water pollution around the river.

Pollution will not go away on its own. Each person must take action to stop it. Every effort to fight pollution, big or small, makes a difference in our world!

GLOSSARY

acid (A-sud) Something that breaks down matter faster than water does.

atoms (A-temz) The smallest parts of any element. Elements are the most basic kind of matter.

batteries (BA-tuh-reez) Things in which energy is stored.

chemicals (KEH-mih-kulz) Matter that can be mixed with other matter to cause changes.

energy (EH-nur-jee) The power to work or to act.

filters (FIL-turz) Things that keep unwanted things from getting in or out.

fuel (FYOOL) Something used to make warmth or power.

lungs (LUNGZ) The parts of an air-breathing animal that take in air.

nutrients (NOO-tree-unts) Food that a living thing needs to live and grow.

program (PROH-gram) A group that does something.

radioactive (ray-dee-oh-AK-tiv) Giving off rays of light, heat, or energy.

recycling (ree-SY-kling) Using something again in a different way.

scientists (SY-un-tists) People who study the world.

water vapor (WAH-ter VAY-pur) The gaseous state of water.

INDEX

WEB SITES

Due to the changing nature of Internet links, PowerKids Press has developed an online list of Web sites related to the subject of this book. This site is updated regularly. Please use this link to access the list: www.powerkidslinks.com/ourpl/pollute/